Heaven's Spectrum

KIRKLYN B. JOHNSON

PUBLISHER
JohnsonTrax Productions & Publishing, LLC
Houston, MS

Copyright 2023 By Kirklyn B. Johnson

All rights reserved. This book or any portion thereof may not be reproduced or used in any manner whatsoever without the expressed written permission of the publisher except for the use of brief quotations in a book review or scholarly journal.

To request permission, contact the publisher at:
Johnsonsprogress@gmail.com

First Printing: 2023

Paperback: ISBN 979-8-218-12471-7

JohnsonTrax Productions & Publishing, LLC
Houston, MS 38851
www.unfinishedclay.org

Note: All scripture references are taken from the Holy Bible KJV

Dedication

First and foremost, this book is dedicated to my family. To my mom and dad, I thank you for pushing me daily to be the best person that I can be. I also thank you for supporting me in every aspiration that I desire to go after. I am forever thankful to God for you both. I will always strive to make you Godly proud.

To my twin brother Kirk and my little sister LaSarah, I love you both dearly and you two hold a special place in my heart. If I had to choose two people to be my siblings, I'd choose you both time and time again. The bond we share is priceless.

To my teachers, the village that my parents and I needed so desperately. Just to name a few: Mrs. Peggy Shempert, Mrs. Kristen Goode, Mrs. Kim Sellers, Mrs. Margaret Futral, Mrs. Christy Foster, and the Late Mrs. Leslie McMullen. You all were there in the beginning and can attest to the many trials I've had to endure. Thank you for holding my hand. To every faculty member of Houston School District, I will remember you all forever! Please know that I am grateful to God for each of you!

This book is also dedicated to all parents with autistic children. I'm thankful and honored that God has allowed me to be a ray of hope for you. Lastly, this book is dedicated to all special needs children across the world on the spectrum. I promise to always advocate for you in the best way I know how. That's by using my voice.

I love you all,

Kirklyn

Table of Contents

Heaven's Spectrum vii

Introduction: My Testimony ix
Music: The Key That Unlocked My World 1
A Letter To Parents 5
How I Carry the Diagnosis 9
A Letter To Mothers 13
How My Diagnosis Humbles Me 15
Choosing To Be a Light 21
A Letter To Fathers 25
A Thankful Heart 27
Learning to Cope with the Residue 33
A Letter To Friends 39
A Bright Road Ahead 41
About The Author 45
A Special Favor 47

Kirklyn B. Johnson..vii

Heaven's Spectrum

viii .... Heaven's Spectrum

INTRODUCTION: MY TESTIMONY

Have you ever found yourself trying to figure out the reason why you were hit with certain tests and trials? Have you ever struggled to figure out what it was that God was trying to show you through specific circumstances? As Christians, it is very common to ponder those questions. However, what if I told you that spiritually there's a bigger purpose behind every trauma, pain, and storm you faced? What if I also told you that connected to every storm you encountered and survived could be the answer or motivation needed to help someone else later in life?

Over the course of my life, God has shown me through autism that ministry is birthed out of things that He allows me to grow through. I have a unique testimony that I'd like to share for the Glory of God because He alone worked a miracle for my family and me. This testimony will also provide a foundation for this book so that you can understand exactly why I titled this book Heaven's Spectrum.

I was born on January 31, 2003. I have a twin brother as well. My parents often state that my brother and I had the longest fingers they'd ever seen on newborns. Other than that, we looked perfect. We were born at 36 ½ weeks gestation which was good for twins. Mom and Dad said we cried a lot... but that's normal for newborns, right? Days and months began to pass, and we began to grow physically. The problem was that despite growing physically, we both were missing cognitive and motor milestones left and right. At the age of 6 months old we still had to be held while sitting because we were unable to sit up. We couldn't pull up, babble, or hold our bottles. In addition, many of the normal infant milestones we were unable to do, or we were severely behind. My dad told me that they even had a game that they made up whenever they'd run into family and friends. The game was called, "Can you make Kirklyn smile?" This was because I had a blank facial expression most of the time, and I didn't respond to the common goo-goo's, gah-gah's, and baby babble that adults attempted. Most of all, my parents stated that the crying was almost constant. Time kept elapsing and we grew further behind. We started walking at 15 months old. We both were still nonverbal. At the age of 2, we were still nonverbal and in diapers. Three years elapsed and it was apparent that something was wrong. This was more than just "needing time to catch up." My parents finally decided to look further into this matter, and they were taken aback by what they would soon find out.

In October of 2006, my parents took us to clinical psychiatrists in order to get official information on what was going on with us. My dad took my brother to a clinic in Starkville, MS, and he was tested for cognitive abilities. My brother scored so low on the test that he scored barely above the mental retardation line. The doctor looked at my dad and stated, "If I were you, I WOULD NOT expect a miracle! Your sons will probably never talk nor understand." While that doctor was speaking, God spoke the scripture Isaiah 53:1 to my dad, and He asked him, "Whose report will you believe?" My dad states that at that moment he knew that faith in God was his only option, and he left the office deciding to believe God despite of the bad report he had just received. I was being tested in another county. My mom states that I was only able to perform very little things and that I repeated words I heard randomly without any rhyme or reason. Needless to say that in the month of October in 2006, my brother and I both received the official diagnosis of Low Functioning Autism due to being nonverbal, socially inadequate, and cognitively impaired. Sounds pretty bad huh? Yeah, it sounds bad to me too! Don't worry because it gets better.

Here is the miracle that overshadows the previous paragraph. One thing that I love about my mom and dad is that they were very active in our local church, and their faith in God was consistent. Even though raising twins with low functioning autism was a challenge, they kept us in service. Man, I love church and even with the diagnosis of autism and being nonverbal, the music in the church mesmerized me! I ESPECIALLY loved the drums. Mom states that in hindsight, church was the only place that we did not do excessive crying. Anyway, one night after a revival service we came home, and my parents state that night the ride home was unusually quiet. My brother and

I did not cry any on the way home which was very unusual for us. When we got home, they placed us in our bedroom. My parents stayed up in the living room for a while because my brother and I would normally cry for hours before we could go to sleep, and they would have to come into our room to console us. We were pretty jolly this night they stated, and they noticed weird babbling sounds coming from our bedroom a little before midnight. Dad states that he and mom tiptoed down the hall to see exactly what my brother and I were doing. They stated that what they discovered nearly floored them. When they peeped into our bedroom, they found my brother and me jumping up and down on our bunkbeds, and we both were saying our first words miraculously! One of us was saying Hallelujah, and my brother (or myself) was replying by saying THANK YOU JESUS! We both were mimicking what we had previously heard that night in revival. From nonverbal to talking suddenly! It was indeed a miracle that we so desperately needed, and it's forever TO GOD BE THE GLORY!

In layman's terms, autism is a disorder that may affect or hinder a person's communication and social skills. The sensory system may also be affected as well. Autism can range from low functioning to high functioning when it comes to measuring a person's ability. Therefore, the term Autism Spectrum Disorder (ASD) is the diagnosis used to identify persons who have these identifiable traits. According to the CDC report from 2021, 1 out of 44 children are diagnosed and placed on the spectrum. This number has quickly increased because in 2006 the CDC reported approximately 1 out of 110 were diagnosed on the spectrum. What I'm getting at is as the years pass, individuals being diagnosed with autism have been growing statistically at a fast and alarming rate. That's truly something to think about! More so, we should also think about how to interact with and integrate the growing population of unique individuals such as myself and my brother into society to be productive citizens! This is easier said than done though. I'll explain my thought process.

In the natural, it is normal for someone to place limitations on individuals with special needs and diagnoses. In some people's opinion, based on the label of autism, a person like me should not have the successes, victories, and experiences that God has allowed me to have. When many hear, "He has autism," it oftentimes makes a person think of limitations and disabilities. Truth be told, the only disabilities I've ever been aware of were the ones that people made me aware of. What I mean by that is, I honestly didn't feel "disabled" even when I exhibited certain traits. I literally had to figure out how to deal with other's expectations or lack thereof. That was my biggest hinderance. I had to deal with "label chains" that were automatically placed upon me because of the diagnosis. I thank God that I've acquired the keys to free myself from man's bondage.

For the past 15 years, I've learned to see myself on another spectrum. This spectrum is not defined by autism, and it has no limitations based on a diagnosis. Overall, I learned to see myself within Heaven's spectrum. That is where I've learned to soar, abide, and thrive.

The purpose of this book is to offer hope to the readers as well as to share lessons learned through my life's experiences while living with the label of autism. You may be surprised to know that we are more "normal" than the world gives us credit for being.

Notes/Thoughts

CHAPTER ONE

Music: The Key That Unlocked My World

> *When it came down to it, music just so happened to be the method that was needed for me to grow into the person that I am today. Was the method weird? Maybe. However, it worked!*
>
> KBJ

If there is one integral part of my life that has helped me tremendously, it is music. Although I was unable to talk due to autism, I've always been able to sing. I come from a long line of singers and preachers on both sides of my family. Due to the diagnosis, it was hard for me to learn simple things such as my numbers and my letters. Nothing else could make those things click or anything for that matter ... except music. I can't explain it, but music somehow literally became a world that made sense.

As a kid, and still to this day, the genre of music that I listen to the most is gospel. It didn't matter the style: traditional, contemporary, gospel rap, southern, quartet...I just love gospel music. Apparently, my mom noticed and figured out that I responded to music differently that I did anything else. Therefore, she began to use music to help me learn basic things I needed to know. She would remix gospel songs and change the lyrics by inserting numbers and alphabets. Strangely, music somehow helped me with every learning obstacle I would face. I struggled with learning in school, and I had a very difficult time learning the lessons being taught. I couldn't comprehend by reading study guides and study notes. I used the method my mom used when she taught me, and I would sing the study guides in song form or preach the notes in sermon topics in order to retain the material. My dad is a pastor, so preaching was not foreign in the house, and I'd literally preach and sing any and everything growing up. It could simply be the weather, days of the week, or something as simple as sweeping the floor. I'd preach or sing about it in order to learn how to do it. It never dawned on me in my wildest dreams that God would use that learning method as I begin to study the Bible. He was preparing me to preach. I preached my first sermon on February 9, 2020.

When it comes down to it, music just so happened to be the key method that was needed for me to grow into the person that I am today. Was it a weird method? Maybe. However, it worked. It may seem foolish in man's eyes, but the Bible states that the foolishness of God is wiser than men. One thing that I want to say to the person reading this book is always go to God for directions on how to handle this thing called life. God instructed us in Proverbs chapter 3 verse 6 to acknowledge Him in all our ways. He promised to direct our paths. Even if His directions are not what you "think" (in your own reasonings) they should be, it would be beneficial for you to obey and follow His path. It's better for you in the long run. His way may require you to lose friends, face opposition, or even isolation. Take comfort in knowing there is always a blessing included in the cost. It will help you to grow into the person that God wants you to be.

Notes/Thoughts

_____
_____
_____
_____
_____
_____
_____
_____
_____
_____
_____
_____
_____

A Letter To Parents

Dear Parents and Guardians,

Please allow me grace and space to sincerely speak with you for a moment. Some of you may be parents of an autistic child. I want to share some things that I feel helped me tremendously. I do understand that all children are different, yet you may be able to use this general advice as reference points as you prayerfully figure out what's specifically necessary for your child. All the following things helped me to become the person that I am today.

The first thing I suggest is to invest in your child. Any gift or passion that they exhibit is worth investing in. I can honestly say that every passion my brother and I had my parents found a way to invest to the best of their resources and abilities. I've stimmed (repetitive clicking motion) with my fingers since an early age. I would click my fingers on any hard surface available to create noise, and as I grew older, I could keep rhythmic beats. I could do that motion for hours, and it calmed me in a sense. My first sign of being advanced in rhythm was at the age of 1. I used pots, pans, and empty boxes to beat on as drums. When my parents discovered that I loved drumming on things, they purchased a mini drum set, and that was the beginning of many investments for me to perfect my gift. If your child exhibits talents or certain preoccupations, consider thinking outside the box and look for ways to invest in what they love. I am a firm believer that the sacrifice of your investment will in return be a blessing to you!

Secondly, encourage your child(ren) to be the best version of themselves. My parents always challenged me to be good at what I set out to do. That extra encouragement made me feel like someone was believing in me, and I tried to rise to the occasion to the best of my abilities.

With that being said, once you understand what your child can tolerate, never compare their progress with anyone else's, and make sure that you incorporate having fun into their lives. So many times it's easy to get tunnel vision on what all they are not doing to where it becomes overwhelming. Nevertheless, don't shy away from having fun. Sometimes sensory limitations must be considered, and that's understandable. Nevertheless, kids like to have fun. Research places that are autism friendly environments and let your child explore. I was raised in a church setting, but my parents made sure that there was a balance between church and normal activities. Anything that your child loves doing whether it's running in circles, lining up cars, or just sitting in the middle of the floor spinning a car wheel, engage the best way you can. Enter their world sometimes. You may be surprised just how peaceful it is just to engage in their world instead of trying to constantly pull them into your present expectations.

Don't be afraid or ashamed to take your child out in public. If they can tolerate public environments, let them see other places and spaces. You may have to accommodate them by investing in noise reducing headphones or other sensory reducing gear, but it's worth it. People are going to be people, and unfortunately you can't control their opinions. If someone is bothered by your child's actions due to autism, that is their issue. If you need to readjust or even leave due to outbursts and interruptions, that's ok. Don't allow those moments to defeat you! The main thing that you should be focused on is the safety and well-being of your child. Anything outside of that is not your responsibility.

One other thing that I feel is important is to always make sure you are giving your child the grace to grow. You cannot rush future breakthroughs into present moments. Growth takes time. Flowers do not grow the moment you plant them. Food is not done the moment you turn your stove on. Sometimes the wait may seem long but know that there is a blessing and reward included in the wait.

Lastly, give your child(ren) a safe space to be themselves. I'm 20 years old at this present moment, and home has always been my safe space. Every time I leave for college, I always look forward to returning home. The reason why I enjoy going home is because my parents and siblings allow me to be myself in my most authentic form. I never have to worry about chaos or being judged. They understand me 100 percent. Making home a safe space for your child(ren) allows them to have room for unhindered growth.

Again, I do understand that every child falls differently on the spectrum, and this is general advice. These are just things that I know helped and still help me tremendously. Keep in mind that I am not an outside researcher or scholar that's throwing out random suggestions. I was the one on the receiving end of everything I've stated WHILE being nonverbal. My language didn't take off instantly either. I had tantrums, a temper, and frequent meltdowns! Nevertheless, I kept growing and now I'm writing this to you! I pray that as you continue to read this book, you see things from a different level of faith. Even though you may be waiting for certain milestones to happen, please keep waiting with a heart of expectancy. Your love, support, expectations, and encouragements are fuel for our lives. Anything can happen at any moment. I'm proof of that statement. Keep up the good work!

Love Always,

Kirklyn

CHAPTER TWO

HOW I CARRY THE DIAGNOSIS

"

I eventually got over my fear of how people would view me, and I embraced how God made me!

KBJ

I find it a blessing and an honor that many people have been blessed through my testimony. Truth be told, there was a time when I hated living with the label of being "autistic." The reason being is that I feared the diagnosis would hinder my relationships with friends and others. I also cringed at the thought of people viewing me differently once they found out. I never wanted pity. As a matter of fact, I personally never felt like something was "wrong." I didn't want people to treat me differently than they treated others. I wanted the same chances and opportunities to prove that I was just as "normal" as other young people. I loved God, and I loved trying to make new friends. Granted, I may have gone about my efforts of communicating differently, but I was whole heartedly trying. Here is what a lot of people fail to realize about others with diagnoses and special needs. WE ALL HAVE A HEART that's made of flesh and blood. Our hearts can be hurt, disappointed, or broken by actions and rejection. We are not exempt from feeling pain. We can read facial expressions and body language. We feel emotions too. Never assume that just because a person's communication is hindered that it applies to their ability to feel and interpret.

As I got older, I realized that the problem was not the people nor the label. The problem was my failure to see the ministry BEHIND the label. I failed to shift my focus on how my story gave hope to others who knew someone or may be dealing with autism themselves. Once I realized this truth, I eventually got over my fear of how people would view me. I embraced how God made me.

God tells us in Psalms 139 verse 14 that we are fearfully and wonderfully made by Him. Let me take a moment to encourage you and know that I am speaking from personal experience and with a sincere heart. The way that God made you is unique and serves a specific purpose. You do not have to walk in fear of people's opinions. Know that God loves you and what HE says about you is the only valid opinion that carries defining weight.

Furthermore, do not allow the enemy room to speak negative things to you. He will try to make you give up hope and live in disappointment and despair. Who is he to say that the different challenges God allowed you to face do not serve a specific, God-designed purpose? The scripture even promises us in Romans 8:28 that ALL things work together for the good of them who love God and are called according to His purpose. One thing I've come to know about God is He is a God of purpose ON PURPOSE. No trial or storm is ever in vain or wasted. My hope is that after reading this chapter, you always keep in mind that the tests and trials of your life that God allows to come to you are a ministry to others. Because of that fact alone, you should hold your head up and believe in yourself. If someone judges you for something beyond your control, then that's a person that does not deserve you anyway. Autism is not a badge of honor in my life, yet it's a valid ministry of my life. On Heaven's spectrum, I know that according to Philippians 2:9 that God exalted His son Jesus to the highest place and gave him the name that is above EVERY name; that at the name of Jesus every knee should bow, in heaven and on earth and under the earth! Fortunately, autism has a name. That means that it must bow when I live on Heaven's spectrum. That's how I carry the diagnosis. I don't deny it, but I place it where it belongs. There is room for whatever you face to be placed under subjection to the mighty name of Jesus! All I know is that it's working for me.

A Letter To Mothers

Dear Moms,

Now that I've talked about how parents are vital to the growth of an autistic child as a unit, I would like to share with you how your love and strength is life changing to us. First, I want to thank God for each of you. There is literally no love in the earth like a mother's love. Secondly, I want to say that you are doing a good job and none of this is your fault. Continue to love like only you can. Even if there is no verbal response, exciting expression, or amazing reaction shown by your child(ren) in return, they know Momma's love is the best hands down. Trust me!

One important suggestion I'd like to share is for you to keep an open mind and be creative. It doesn't matter how silly or goofy something is, and if it grabs your child's attention, go with it! I can envision my mom even when I was nonverbal, and she would stomp through the house making silly songs. I mentioned earlier in this book about how I learned my numbers and letters by her remixing gospel songs. My brother and I rarely understood the words in the early stages. We just remember giggling and liking the vibrations from her stomping on the floor. Every little bit matters. Hone in to what they are good at and engage whenever you can. Being creative also allows a child to explore different options.

Celebrate small victories. I don't care how small or trivial you may think they are. Take a moment to celebrate. Positive reactions give clues to appropriate behaviors. Keep note of when your child reaches milestones and continue to show unconditional love. Unconditional love really matters. Hugs, kisses, and loving words to an autistic child can really make them feel like they matter. Additionally, speak positive words to them and expect greatness from them. Proverbs chapter 18 verse 21 states that life and death are in the power of the tongue. As the mother, it is vital that you tell your child(ren) that they are smart and have a unique identity. Help your child(ren) focus on what they are great at, and brag on them in that area. That builds confidence.

The world may place your child in a labeled box. Please make sure that you use your voice and advocate for them until they can speak for themselves. I learned early that even though I may go about a thing differently, I still deserve the chance to try. With that being said, my final advice would be to never give up on your child. It may be exhausting at times, but don't stop dreaming for them! We have the potential to do amazing things. Most times you are the first to figure out what that amazing superpower is! Mom, you are phenomenal, and I appreciate you!

Love Always,

Kirklyn

CHAPTER THREE

How My Diagnosis Humbles Me

"

*I always try to make sure that whatever I accomplish in life,
I give honor and glory to God.*

KBJ

In 20 years of life, God has graced me to obtain multiple achievements, accomplishments, and accolades. I say that with great joy and in awe of His awesome power. You see, If God declares a thing over your life, NOTHING (NO-THING) can stop it from coming to pass. I remember last year my mom asked me a very direct question one afternoon during one of our many conversations. She asked, "Son, do you remember being nonverbal?" I sat for a minute and pondered on how to respond. I'd never given much thought about what I remembered until that moment. Right then and there my mind swiftly began to recall things, and I had vivid memories of my young childhood flash in my mind. Frustration and sadness entered my heart briefly because I could vividly see my twin brother and me. Both of us were unable to talk. I could feel an indescribable pain in my stomach by just thinking about what Mom asked. Here is the thing that enlightened me the most. Our brain was processing things correctly while being unable to express things verbally. I began to tell my mom stories with many details of my accounts of what happened in certain settings during our nonverbal years. I couldn't verbalize them then, but the memories were and are still present today. Therefore, I began to tell my parents everything (good and bad). I remember Mom sitting at the table in tears while listening to me recall the past. She stated, "Kirklyn, I knew it! You were always understanding even when it seemed like you weren't." Apparently, I just had to catch up verbally to what I was always feeling. When I learned to articulate my emotions, a lot of my outbursts and frustrations ceased. Although I'm 20 years old, I've only been verbal for 16 years of the 20.

God has allowed me to be on academic honor roll since 7th grade until even now in college. I was a part of the High School Student Council. I was chosen to be drumline captain for two consecutive years for our high school band. I graduated with honors and received several scholarships to further my education. I am the Co-Producer and percussionist for our family's business JohnsonTrax Productions. I was also blessed to launch my own clothing brand, KBJ ChristianWear on January 11, 2021. I listed all those things just to say that I'd have none of them without God. I simply choose to never let anything I do or obtain to bring glory to myself. I am compelled to give glory to God for everything. I purposefully keep in my mind that I would not be doing as well as I am without God, and here is my reason for saying that.

In Deuteronomy chapter 8, scripture tells the story of how the children of Israel were getting ready to enter and possess their Promised Land. However, God told them not to forget Him and His commandments after they received the promise and blessings. God basically said that IF they failed to keep his commandments, He would take away their blessings and allow their promised land to be taken by their enemies. Sometimes we can become so preoccupied with how blessed we are to the point where we forget the one who blessed us in the first place. I refuse to forget God and whenever the temptation to be prideful presents itself, I remember that first and foremost it was GOD who opened my mind and understanding and blessed me with the ability to obtain the blessings I have at this moment. It's because of His grace and His mercies that I am doing as well as I am today.

We should never think so highly of ourselves to where there is no room for God to get Glory from our lives. Remind yourselves daily that every blessing, achievement, and platform that He graciously bestows upon you can also be taken away! Many people started low on the spectrum and remained there. My heart will forever have a soft spot for them as I was once there as well! I've had to take ADHD medication just to focus. I know what it feels like to desire to participate in social activities but not completely understanding the full dynamics of how to fit in or articulate how I feel. I know what all that feels like, and God delivered me by his power! I don't know in-depth medically how the autistic brain functions and triggers, but I DO know that it's possible to regress. That reason alone humbles me. I haven't visited Heaven as the Apostle Paul did, but I'm proud to say that I can at least view life from Heaven's spectrum.

Notes/Thoughts

CHAPTER FOUR

Choosing To Be a Light

"

The biggest ministry that you have is the way you carry yourself as well as how you treat others.

KBJ

Matthew 5:16 tells us that every Christian should let their light shine bright before men, that they may see our good works, and glorify God which is in Heaven. In today's society, you will come across many people with different personalities. That's the way God designed us. We are all different, and that's a good thing. The world has a lot of mean-spirited people in it, but I choose not to be in that number. You never know what a person is going through behind closed doors or in life in general. Every single day I strive to be a positive light to everyone I meet. I've been like that since I was little. I will identify myself as being an extrovert. Because of that I do not struggle with meeting new people, therefore being friendly is no problem at all. Quite oddly, I love hugs as well.

With that being said, I have always looked at the word "successful" differently, and I've acquired my own definition. The world see success as having wealth, fame, a good family, fine houses, and cars. However, my definition of success is living a God-filled life while leaving a legacy of love and memories that impact future generations. When I leave this world, I want the peace of knowing that I've made a Godly impact on the people I was surrounded by. That's what success means and looks like to me. I'm forever grateful to God for opening my mind as well as expanding my vocabulary, and I strive to share every gift within me to show Christlike love to everyone I meet. More importantly, whenever an opportunity is presented, I seize the moment to share God's word.

There is a story in the Bible where it talks about how Jesus sat with the publicans and the sinners. When the Pharisees saw him, they asked Jesus why was he sitting with them? Jesus answered them and said that he was not come to call the righteous, but sinners to repentance. I try to make that statement a staple in my thoughts to understand I am a living ministry. So many people get the misconception that ministry is just something revolved around church and church activities. That's not the case. Ministry is so much more than just doing. Ministry is also "being." The biggest ministry you will ever display is your life and character. That is the first light (or lack thereof) a person encounters. Which type of ministry do you choose to display? There are people in our midst who have dealt with traumatic experiences. Those experiences could have derived from hurt, judgement, or just walking around feeling rejected. Life may have dealt them some cruel cards, and they are not sure how to move forward. How cool would it be to know that you could possibly be the bridge that God uses to lead that person to Christ his ONLY begotten son! Someone close to you needs your love and kindness. They benefit greatly from your encouragement. Whether you realize it or not, someone is hanging on to life because you said, "You're needed in this world" or, "You're doing a good job." Those words of kindness may open the door for you to tell them about the love of Jesus. What I'm trying to say is whenever you have an opportunity, use it to show the love of Christ. Choose to be a light because someone needs to see it!

Notes/Thoughts

_____
_____
_____
_____
_____
_____
_____
_____

A Letter To Fathers

Dear Dads,

Fathers play an influential part in their child(ren)'s life. I want to share from my point of view ways that fathers can help their autistic child(ren). The first thing I'll say is that your leadership matters the most. Fathers set the tone and anchor the emotions of the family. Although my mom played important roles in my learning, God used the faith of my father to build upon as a foundation. It was my father that refused to agree with the doctor as he stated, "Don't expect a miracle." My dad had two choices: 1. To not expect a miracle or 2. To wake up daily looking for miracles to be performed. I'm glad he chose option 2. Being a fervent leader matters while raising a child with autism. It is equally important for you to be someone your child can mimic. Whether you believe it or not, your child is watching everything that you do. We (my brother and I) picked up on some of the smallest things our dad did in everyday life. That's how we learned a lot of character and social traits. We mimicked him even when we didn't understand. Now, we mimic him just to joke with him mockingly, but he was and still is our example. He was water and we were sponges. We soaked up many of his behaviors. As your child(ren) grow, they will do the same from you.

Another thing that is important is for you to be emotionally available to your child(ren). Moms give the best hugs and kisses, but dads give the best confidence. That starts our emotionally stability. When our worlds are falling apart or we are fresh in a meltdown, you just being available helps. There were many nights our dad sat by our bedside just rubbing our heads so that we could calm down. We didn't understand a whole lot, but we knew in our minds that when we cried, dad was coming to sit with us. I wish we could have verbalized it, but that was our signal. We needed our dad. Your child(ren) need you too.

Above all, make sure you are speaking the word of God to and over your child. I understand that everyone has different beliefs and thoughts concerning this, but all I know is that it was a game changer for my brother and me. Before we were born, my dad would read to us bible stories while we were in mom's belly. He also would proclaim Isaiah 53:5 believing that we were healed. The bible tells us in Isaiah 40:8 that the grass withers, and the flowers fade: but the word of God lasts forever. Even if your child cannot articulate using words, still use THE WORD. It does nothing but strengthen your faith… it's still beneficial. I appreciate you dads!

Love Always,

Kirklyn

A Thankful Heart

> *I have no complaints against God! Especially when I view him through the lens of a thankful heart!*
>
> KBJ

The greatest lesson I've learned since overcoming this diagnosis is to never take anything for granted. Every blessing that God has given is priceless. Even the smallest things bring gratefulness into my heart. A lot of things that others call common is a miracle in my life. Being verbal as well as being able to articulate correctly what I'm thinking and feeling makes my heart so happy! Why? It is because the odds were stacked against me and not for me at one time. God tipped the scale in my favor! For that I'm grateful.

Having a routine is not uncommon for children on the spectrum. As a matter of fact, I thrive best with routines and schedules. Every morning I start my day with prayer and reading the Bible. That is the most important part of my morning. When I pray, I begin with gratitude and thankfulness. I tell God "Thank You" EVERY DAY for the ability to talk, understand, and for the use of my limbs. I thank Him for the ability to make friends. I thank Him for being able to love as well as feel love and express those emotions. I'm grateful that I know how to walk and tie my shoes. The fact that I can meet my basic needs as well as accomplish other things fills my heart with joy. I know those are minor things, but they are MAJOR things to me. You become grateful when you can do things that you previously couldn't do. I often reflect on the Dr.'s statement to my father back in 2006. The words "Don't expect a miracle" are devastating to think about. I thank God daily that He is a miracle working God. I thank Him for proving the doctor wrong…DAILY!

Over the course of my young life, I've never had a need that God didn't address and take care of. I can even remember in upper elementary school when I was diagnosed with ADHD. I was a very hyper child and focusing on any task for just a few minutes was very hard for me to do. I was placed on medication just to function, but I did not like the way the medicine made me feel. I took it during the months of school in order to focus and learn. I remember hearing my dad preach one Sunday, and he stated that "God can do the impossible if you can supply the faith." I prayed that night for God to help me focus so that I could come off the medication. By the 7th grade, I no longer had to take the medication. My grades increased, and I started being on honor roll my 7th grade year. I'm blessed to say that I remained on honor roll all through high school and was able to graduate with special honors. I began college this past fall at Northeast Mississippi Community College, and I entered the semester owing nothing. Everything was covered by multiple scholarships. I am not stating this from a boastful standpoint, but I am stating this from a thankful heart.

In life, it's so easy to focus on what's wrong when we should turn our hearts to meditate on all the things that are right! There are things that I could choose to magnify by wishing they were better or by wishing I could do what someone else is doing greater. Why would I disrespect God in that manner? I say that because in the natural if you have a child that you have given your best, but they still complain and constantly remind you of what someone has better… It can seem as if they are not content and thankful for what they already have. I see it the same way in the spiritual realm. It's disrespectful to desire other's lives, gifts, and talents when God has blessed you with a plethora of amazing gifts already! It's called coveting. Instead of looking over the fence, I thank God for the piece of ground on which I'm able to stand! I always try to end my prayer with thankfulness to God by telling Him that if He does not do another thing in my life, He has already done well, and He has done enough. I have no complaints against God, ESPECIALLY when I view him through the lens of a thankful heart!

    Take a moment to reflect on your life. What all are you thankful for? When was the last time you considered all the blessings that God has already bestowed upon you? Never allow the stresses of life to cause you to be ungrateful. Even if things didn't go so well at times, be grateful that you survived those moments. I'm aware of the fact that I'm only 20 years old. I know that someone reading this has gone through some horrendous tests and trials. I don't discredit that fact. Here is what I will say. My job is not to compare levels of the struggles. My job is to THANK GOD that He causes us to have victory over the struggles. Truth be told, there are some who wish they had the problems you face simply because their situation is worse. For that fact, I choose to thank God for it all. I cannot say that if I had a chance to start my life over that I would choose to deal with autism. I am certain that God has changed my life and those in my immediate surroundings through the spectrum. I was ashamed at one point, but now I'm not. I even feel that being on the spectrum has kept me away from certain situations, certain crowds, and certain negative influences. Romans 8:28 states that ALL things work together for good to those who love God, to those who are called according to His purpose. I'm sure that a lot of my teachers thought about quitting daily because of challenges on their job. However, I'm thankful that they didn't retire or quit before they taught me. I needed every one of them in some form or fashion. It's the little things such as that revelation that makes my heart so grateful. God knew that I needed consistency in every aspect of my life. God allowed me to have the same principal for 10 of my school years, and the last year he was promoted to School Superintendent! That just blows my mind when I think about that. That literally puts joy in my heart because it provided me with stability and a feeling of safety. My community in which I live is a safe place for me. I've settled into college, and I have amazing friends who accept me just as I am. They allow me to be the authentic Kirklyn Johnson. I have an awesome roommate who is patient with me. He helps me in areas I fall short in, and I love him like a brother! Why would I not view life with a thankful heart? I've had disappointments and challenges, and I know that I will face challenges ahead. What I'm certain of is that God is the same yesterday, today, and forevermore. Since He is Lord of my life, I have nothing to fear. He will take care of me. I choose to live with a thankful heart.

CHAPTER SIX

Learning to Cope with the Residue

"

People who truly love you will deal with you at your lowest without judgement.

KBJ

I believe that one of the greatest ministries you can share with someone is the ministry of transparency. In 2nd Corinthians chapter 12, the scriptures tell of an account with Apostle Paul and how he was blessed to visit Heaven. Right after Paul describes this glorious encounter, he states that he was given a thorn in the flesh (a persistent, annoying problem in his waking life that he could not get rid of). Paul realized that the purpose of his suffering was to keep him mentally grounded and humble as well as for others to not exalt him above measure. Sometimes people can get excited about the *idea* of you instead of accepting the real you. I don't ever want people to exalt my progress, successes, and credentials to the point to where they forget that there are some flaws that God has graced me to live with.

Some of the most well-known people in the Bible that we preach and teach on today had flaws. For example, Moses was a great leader, but he had a speech impediment. Peter was handpicked by Jesus Himself to be a disciple, but he had a temper. Saul was a persecutor of the church and murdered a lot of people, but God chose him to be His Apostle. If we are honest, many of us carry various flaws, but none of us should be judged by them.

Although God has given me victory over autism, I still deal with the residue of it sometimes. Residue can be frustrating. The most frustrating thing I face is when conversating with people, I often take what they say literally. Sometimes it's challenging to know if people are joking with me, being sarcastic, or being serious. To a person with autism, there is no gray area. That's why I try to make sure I explain this to the people I call friends and are close to me. I tell them to mean what they say and say what they mean. That helps me out a lot with understanding appropriately. It's not that I'm ignorant. Words just hit my brain differently, and I process them the way they are said. It's not a deficiency, it's just a different way of analyzing and understanding.

Many times, I have wondered what life would be like if I were different and "normal" as described by society. I used to wonder if I needed to change to fit in. I've come to the peaceful conclusion that God made me just like He fashioned me to be. I am unique, and there is only ONE Kirklyn B. Johnson on the earth. That excites me. I've also learned that the people who truly love me deal with me on my level. They know how I function, and they leave room for me to grow and understand in their presence. They don't make me feel like I'm inadequate or odd. They embrace the gift of me, and I strive to do the same in return. Mainly, I've come to the realization that everyone is not committed to understanding me, and that's ok. Sometimes I'm not their first, second, or even third choice as a friend. It used to make me feel sad, but now it does not bother me as much. Some seasons in life call for walking with Jesus alone. I'm content with that revelation as well. Why am I content? I'm glad you asked. I'm at peace because Jesus sat with 12 disciples at the Passover, but when it came down to His crucifixion, only one was present at the foot of His cross. He didn't have autism or anything wrong with Him, yet He wasn't normal. He had supernatural powers which made him different from the rest. People scrutinize others who are different. Therefore, I'm no exception. I'm ok with that.

What residue do you deal with from time to time? It could be residue from bad choices in life, mistakes of your past, or just emotional trauma from generalized hardships. God will give you grace to carry it without shame and know that those areas in your life do not define you! You are not a label; you are unique and loved by God. According to Philippians chapter 1 verse 6, every good work that God starts, He finishes and completes. As long as you are alive, God will continue to help and mold you into his perfect masterpiece. Whatever residue you may deal with, God is with you, and He is not done with making you better. My family sings a song titled "Unfinished Clay." The words are...

When looking in the mirror, I'll tell you what I see.
A marvelous creation, staring back at me.
But if you stare a little closer, you may want to throw me away.
Truth be told, I'm very valuable. I am unfinished clay!

When you hear me speak, I can't say my words so well.
I may not have the best articulation, by now I know you can tell.
But if you listen with the ears of God, you'll be quite amazed.
I'm pressing on in-spite of it all. I am unfinished clay!

I'm not perfect I have many flaws... I am different and that's OK.
Some days I smile, some days I hide, the potter made me that way.
Handle me very delicately, and please don't throw me away,
Truth be told, I'm very valuable, I am unfinished clay.

So, when you see a person, whose struggle is different than yours,
Know that life is hard and unfair at times, and when it rains it usually pours.
Before you laugh, or push them aside, or criticize them for being that way
Accept them for exactly who they are, and that is unfinished clay!

Residue is not a bad thing my friend. It's just a reminder that leads to a road of humility. I often think of the lame man who laid 38 years at the pool of Bethesda. After a brief encounter with Jesus, he immediately gained strength in his legs and ankles, and he began to walk. I like what Jesus told him during the miracle. He first asked him would he like to be made whole? After giving a few excuses, the lame mane decided that he indeed wanted to be made whole. Jesus told him to pick up his bed and walk. So many people when thinking of that miracle focus only on the walking. I think it's quite unique that Jesus instructed him to carry the bed he was previously confined to instead of leaving it behind. Sometimes, along with the miracle, God wants us to talk about the mess as well. That way you will have proof that you went through those trying times. God is known for making people look so much better than their low circumstances. Sometimes it's necessary to keep what you went through at near grasp. It helps to remember those moments. Humility is a byproduct of remembering.

I may not be where I want to be in life, but I sure thank God that I'm not where I used to be! Regardless of who you are, there is still room for growth and progress. Never give up on yourself or your dreams. We are all a work in progress! Thankfully, we are in the Potter's hand. Don't be ashamed of residue. It's proof that you survived!

A Letter To Friends

Dear Friends,

I'd like to take the time to share with you just how important your friendship means to those who have special needs. Sometimes it's hard to approach you because socially we are unsure how to go about doing so. Sometimes our self-esteem is not that great due to previous rejections. Bullies come in all shapes, forms and fashions, and many of us have suffered at their hands. Nevertheless, we love to have friends. We pick up a lot of social cues from hanging around you. A word of advice is don't be afraid to be friends with those who are different than your normal choices. Reach out to those who sit alone sometimes. I am a firm believer that every person that God allows you to meet is designed for a purpose. Who's to say that he or she couldn't be the most loyal friend you'll ever cross paths with? Additionally, keep in mind that they have feelings too. Granted everyone doesn't have the capacity to be nice, therefore make sure to speak up for those who can't speak up for themselves. Don't allow them to be bullied in your presence. That's not what a real friend does. They may not be able to fully articulate how they feel, but know that they can indeed feel hurt, disappointments, rejections, and emotional pains.

Last, but certainly not least, don't treat your autistic friend (or any friend for that matter) differently from the rest, and allow them to participate to the level of their comfort. Be mindful of their cues of what makes them uncomfortable. Honestly, great friends allow room for growth, and autistic children tend to mimic who they look up to. Always display good behavior and habits in their presence. The goal is to spark growth.

To every person who has befriended me, I want to say that I appreciate and respect you tremendously! It gives me an added strength that I need to thrive. You are helping me daily and I thank each of you!

Love Always,

Kirklyn

CHAPTER SEVEN

A Bright Road Ahead

> *Learn to live on Heaven's Spectrum*
> KBJ

I pray that you were inspired by reading this book. It wasn't a long read, but hopefully it was informative in one aspect or another. As you matriculate through life, know that you can have a positive impact on those you deal with. When you cross paths with others who are different from you, remember to be kind. Never judge someone based on something that they had no control over. Instead, seek to find ways to help them or at least speak up for them if you discover they are being mistreated or wronged.

Your life is a unique journey, and sometimes you follow different paths to your destiny! There is no cookie cutter road map or a one size fits all plan that is set before us. Therefore, we all set out in hopes of finding the path that feels appropriate while praying for the best outcomes. Positive outcomes are sometimes experienced behind negative experiences. Nevertheless, your story and life's journey are unique and built just for you. I know what it feels like to travel in circles while desperately feeling the need to progress. I found the perfect lane for me that led me to thrive on Heaven's Spectrum.

I can truly say in hindsight that God had His hands on me, and He still does. I am enjoying college life, I have great friends, and I'm thriving in ways that man stated I would never do. I am headed towards a career in music education. I chose that major because that's where my strengths are, and I want to make a difference in other children's lives like someone invested in me. Jeremiah 29:11 states that God has a plan and a future for me. My road of life just happened to lead through autism. I've grown and discovered a lot on that road. I don't despise any lessons learned. I feel that I have a unique skill set that was a result of it. I embrace the good and the bad. It has made me who I am, and if nothing else, it has fixed my sight. I'm so blessed to be thriving on Heaven's Spectrum. I'd like to conclude this book by praying for you and your children.

Prayer for parents: God, I come to you in prayer for the parents who have autistic children. I pray that you give them grace to push through every obstacle they face. Whenever they feel like giving up, help them to realize that all things work together for their good. I pray that you give them wisdom on how to handle and raise their child. Help them to be patient, to show love, and help them to know that You are with them every day. Father, lead them through every storm that they face. Help them to trust in You because You do all things well, and You never make any mistakes. Finally, I pray that You will get glory from their lives. In Jesus' name I pray, Amen.

For the children: God, I pray for every autistic child. I first ask that You get the glory out of their lives. Let Your light shine through them each day. Protect them from all hurt, harm, and danger. I pray that You guide their footsteps. Moreover, I pray for healing. One thing I know is that You are no respecter of persons. The same way You touched me, I know that You can heal and touch them too. We believe Your report! All these things I ask in Your son Jesus' name, amen.

Kirklyn B. Johnson..45

About The Author

<u>Minister Kirklyn Johnson</u> is the son of Bishop Stan and Evangelist Shalandor Johnson of Houston, MS. Kirklyn is a 2022 graduate of Houston High School and a current student at Northeast Mississippi Community College in Booneville, MS. He is currently studying Music Education and plans to become a Music Vocal Instructor. Kirklyn launched his clothing brand in 2021: KBJ ChristianWear. He is also co-producer and percussionist for JohnsonTrax Productions, LLC. Kirklyn loves to sing, preach, and write songs in his spare time. He and his family are advocates for Autism Awareness.

Kirklyn Johnson, Author

Kirk Johnson(right) (Twin brother) Executive producer/lead musician of JohnsonTrax Productions, LLC. Kirk works at Houston School District in the music department.

A Special Favor

Dear Readers,

I pray that this book has inspired you in a positive way! Please know that I am not chasing platforms nor clout in any manner. I simply want to be an inspiration. With that in mind, if you feel like what I shared may help someone else, will you please recommend or share this book? Also, will you take a moment to leave a review on Amazon, Barnes and Noble, or any other book site where this book can be purchased? You can share your thoughts and testimonies with me on social media. I'd like to say THANKS in advance for helping me to share my story with the world.

Respectfully,

Kirklyn

www.ingramcontent.com/pod-product-compliance
Ingram Content Group UK Ltd.
Pitfield, Milton Keynes, MK11 3LW, UK
UKHW022241230426
12048UKWH00018BA/1389